DNA & Genetic Engineering

Robert Snedden

Heinemann Library

Chicago, Illinois

Designed by Kimberly R. Miracle and Betsy Wernert
Illustrations by Wooden Ark
Printed and bound in China by Leo Paper Group

12 11 10 09 08
10 9 8 7 6 5 4 3 2 1

New edition ISBNs: 978-1-4329-0032-8 (hardcover)
                     978-1-4329-0039-7 (paperback)

The Library of Congress has cataloged the first edition as follows:
Snedden, Robert.
 DNA & genetic engineering/ Robert Snedden.
    v. cm. -- (Cells and life)
Includes index
Contents: Nature's way -- Reading the manual -- Protein factories -- Gene control -- Introducing e.coli -- Chopping up DNA -- The split gene problem -- Hitting the target -- Bacterial benefits -- Turning to phages again -- Going multicellular -- Nature's genetic engineer -- Designer plants -- Transgenic animals -- Transgenic applications -- Gene therapy -- Stem cells -- The consequences of cloning -- Genome mapping -- Genome challenges
    ISBN 1-58810-674-8 (HC) -- ISBN 1-58810-936-4 (Pbk.)
 1. Genetic engineering--Juvenile literature. 2. DNA--Juvenile literature.
 [1. Genetic engineering. 2. DNA] I. Title: DNA & genetic engineering. II. Title. III. Series.
   QH442 .S62 2002
   572.8'6--dc21
                              2001008591

Acknowledgements
The publishers would like to thank the following for permission to reproduce photographs: Contra Costa Times/Zuma Press p. **41** (Dan Rosenstrauch); Corbis pp. **10** (J. L. Amos), **28** (U. Walz), **43** (Andrew Brookes); Corbis/LWA-Dann Tardif p. **42**; FPG p. **4** (J. Cummins); Powerstock Photo Library p. **38**; Rosenfeld Images Ltd/Photo Researchers, Inc p. **25**; Science Photo Library pp. **31** (M. Baret) (Rapho), **27** (J. Burgess), **23** (M. Fermariello), **40** (S. Fraser), **32** (M. Iwafuji), **21** (J. King-Holmes), **37** (A. Leonard), **12** (K. Lounatmaa), **13** (H. Morgan), **29(t)** (S. Moulds), **5**, **15**, **18** (G. Murti), **36** (Y. Nikas), **20** (D. Parker), **26** (M. Read), **24** (S. Stammers), **39** (G. Tompkinson), **33**, **34** (J. C. Revy), **30** (M. Whitaker); Science Photo Library/Agstock p. **29(b)** (E. Young); Science Photo Library/Biology Media p. **22**; Science Photo Library/Max Planck Institute pp. **14**, **16** (J. Berger); Science Photo Library/Omikron p. **9**; Science Photo Library/University of Pennsylvania Medical Center p. **11** (M. Lewis); The New York Times/Redux p. **35** (Amelia Panico).

Cover photograph of a DNA spiral, reproduced with permission of Michael Dunning/Getty Images.

Our thanks to Richard Fosbery for his comments in the preparation of this book, and also to Alexandra Clayton.

Every effort has been made to contact copyright holders of any material reproduced in this book.
Any omissions will be rectified in subsequent printings if notice is given to the Publisher.

Disclaimer
All the Internet addresses (URLs) given in this book were valid at the time of going to press. However, due to the dynamic nature of the Internet, some addresses may have changed, or sites may have ceased to exist since publication. While the author and publishers regret any inconvenience this may cause readers, no responsibility for any such changes can be excepted by either the author or the publishers.

Contents

Some words are shown in bold, **like this**. You can find
the definitions for these words in the glossary.

Nature's Way

Genetic engineering has been around for more than 30 years, yet it remains a very controversial topic. It is possible to produce crops that are resistant to herbicides, fruits that stay fresher for longer, and rice that can provide hungry people with extra vitamins. But there are many who think that this tinkering with nature carries too many risks. Since the first mammal, Dolly the sheep, was successfully **cloned** in 1997, there has been much discussion about the possibility of cloning humans. As far as we know, no one has managed to do so, and many believe it should never happen. In this book you can learn about some of the techniques used in genetic engineering, and come to your own conclusions about whether or not it is a good thing.

What is a gene?

In the simplest terms, a **gene** is an inherited instruction for a particular characteristic. Each **organism** inherits its genes from its parents. For instance, genes control the color of your eyes and the type of hair you have—whether it is straight or curly, light or dark. Each organism has thousands of genes. Some characteristics are influenced by one or two genes. Eye color, for example, is influenced by just a few different genes. Other characteristics, such as the height of an individual or their intelligence, are the result of the combined effects of many different genes.

Each gene is a part of a very long molecule found in all living cells, called **DNA (deoxyribonucleic acid)**. In cells with a **nucleus** (**eukaryote** cells), DNA is found within the nucleus. When the cell is dividing, the individual DNA molecules coil up to form structures called **chromosomes**.

A child inherits genes from its father and from its mother. The same color eyes or hair as a parent is a result of these genetic connections.

Mutations

Each time a cell divides, it makes a copy of its DNA. On rare occasions a mistake is made and part of the DNA molecule is copied incorrectly. These mistakes in the DNA molecule are called **mutations**. Altered, or mutated, genes can be passed on from a parent to its children.

Most times these changes are small and don't matter much—it would be as if you misspelled a single word in a set of instructions and no one noticed. Other times, however, the change might alter the entire meaning of a genetic instruction, with the result that the gene does something entirely different. The result may be disastrous, leading to the death of the organism. Then again, the change might be harmless—such as producing straight instead of curly hair. On rare occasions, the change gives an advantage. An animal might be able to run faster, for example, and escape from its predators.

The chromosomes (orange) are clearly visible in the centre of the dividing cell. In non-dividing cells, the chromosomes are not visible. Magnification approx. x 4,000.

Random shuffling

We all have a different set of genes that play a role in making us who we are. You will have characteristics in common with your parents, and your brothers and other close relatives because you have many genes in common, but in each person the mix of genes is different. Only identical twins have exactly the same set of genes.

On the whole, everyone has two versions of each gene, one from each parent. Males and females each produce sex cells—cells that contain only one version of each gene. When these sex cells form, there is some shuffling of the genes. The genes in the parent's chromosomes are mixed into new combinations.

A male and a female sex cell combine in a process called fertilization. The fertilized cell—the first cell of a new living thing—once again has two sets of genes, one from each parent. Fertilization is a random event. There is no plan as to which male and female sex cells will successfully combine to form a new living thing.

The possible number of combinations that can arise from gene shuffling and random fertilization is truly mind-boggling. There are 10^{600} possible gene combinations that can occur in humans. That is a 1 with 600 zeroes after it. Part of what genetic engineering is about is taking the randomness out of the gene shuffling and taking control of which genes appear in a particular organism. Before we get to that, we'll take a closer look at how genes actually work.

2 Reading the Manual

A cell's **DNA** can be thought of as an instruction manual—a set of instructions for making parts of a cell. Each **gene** is the plan for a specific part. The parts that genes carry instructions for are called **proteins**. If the instruction written in a gene is activated, a protein is created.

cell

nucleus

P Phosphate
S Sugar
A Adenine
G Guanine
C Cytosine
T Thymine

} bases

DNA double helix

The structure of the DNA molecule.
DNA is made up of two long chains of
nucleotides connected at regular intervals
and twisted to form a double helix.

Proteins are the building blocks and workhorses of the cell. Some proteins are parts of the cell structure. Others are **enzymes**. Enzymes are **catalysts** that control chemical reactions in the cell. Each reaction in the cell has its own specific enzyme, and because the enzymes control the reactions, they effectively control the cell and the way it develops.

These events at the level of the cell give rise to the characteristics we see in the **organism**, such as pink flowers on a pea plant, or curly hair on a child. This process of carrying out a gene's instructions is called **gene expression**.

A cell doesn't act on all its DNA instructions at once. Different genes are turned on and off when they are needed. This is because DNA isn't just a small instruction manual—it's a cellular encyclopedia. You never read an encyclopedia from cover to cover, you only read those articles that you need at a particular time. In a multi-cellular organism, such as a plant or an animal, all the cells (except the sex cells we mentioned earlier) contain the same DNA. However, there are many different types of cells, and different genes are turned on in each cell type. Every cell in an organism has the same instruction manual, but different cells are reading different parts of it.

DNA and proteins

We have seen that the goal of carrying out a gene's instruction is to make a protein. Protein molecules are long chains, made up of small subunits called **amino acids**. There are about 20 different kinds of amino acids. A single chain of amino acids is called a **polypeptide**. A protein may have just one polypeptide, or it may have several connected together.

The order of the amino acids in a polypeptide chain is important. Replacing one type of amino acid with another can affect the way the protein works. This is why it is so important for the cell to follow the instructions for each protein in its DNA.

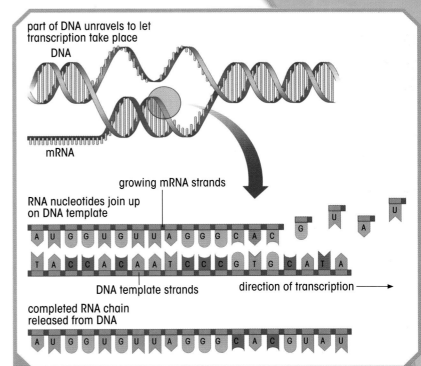

Transcribing a section of DNA to make a messenger RNA molecule. The enzyme RNA polymerase joins the RNA nucleotides together to form a single molecule. Transcription happens very quickly: about 30 new nucleotides are added to the chain each second.

A gene's instructions are written in the structure of the DNA molecule. DNA is made up of two long chains of smaller molecules called **nucleotides**. It looks something like a spiraled, twisted ladder with the two chains wound around each other. Chemicals called **bases** connect the strands together at regular intervals. The order of the bases carries the genetic instructions.

There are four different bases: adenine (A), cytosine (C), guanine (G), and thymine (T). The bases pair up across the molecule, like rungs on a ladder. T is always paired with A, and G with C. The two DNA chains are said to be complementary because the sequence of bases on one strand determines the sequence on the other.

Copying a gene

When a cell wants to make a particular protein, it first has to copy the instructions from the DNA. Copying a gene is called **transcription**. When a gene is being transcribed, the DNA molecule unwinds at the spot where that gene is located. One strand of the DNA, called the coding strand, acts as a template for making another molecule, called **RNA (ribonucleic acid)**. RNA is very similar to DNA, but it is made up of a single strand of bases, not a double strand. Also, one of the bases in DNA, thymine (T), is replaced by another base called uracil (U). This RNA transcript is called **messenger RNA**. It will carry the protein-building instructions from the **nucleus** to the **cytoplasm**, where the actual assembly of bases takes place.

Protein Factories

The next stage in making a protein is called **translation**. The order of the **bases** along the **RNA** strand will be translated into a series of amino acids to be assembled into a **polypeptide** chain.

But how can just four bases carry instructions for 20 different amino acids? The answer is that the bases have to be read in groups of three. Each group of three bases, called a triplet or **codon**, represents a specific amino acid. There are 64 possible codons that can be made using four bases. Each amino acid is coded for by one or more of these codons. The amino acid lysine, for instance, can be coded as either AAA or AAG. The complete amino acid dictionary is what we call the **genetic code**. The genetic code is the same in all living **organisms**, a fact that is of great importance in genetic engineering.

Reading the code

The actual process of building proteins takes place in structures in the **cytoplasm** called **ribosomes**. A ribosome attaches itself to one end of the **messenger RNA** strand, then moves along it, reading it codon by codon, and translating the instructions to build a polypeptide.

Another type of RNA, called **transfer RNA**, plays a vital part in the assembly. There are different forms of transfer RNA, each of which carries a particular amino acid. A particular transfer RNA molecule will bind only to the messenger RNA codon that corresponds to the amino acid it carries. For example, a transfer RNA carrying lysine might only bind to the codon AAA.

This illustration shows how proteins (developing polypeptide chains) are assembled on a ribosome. The messenger RNA is translated by transfer RNA.

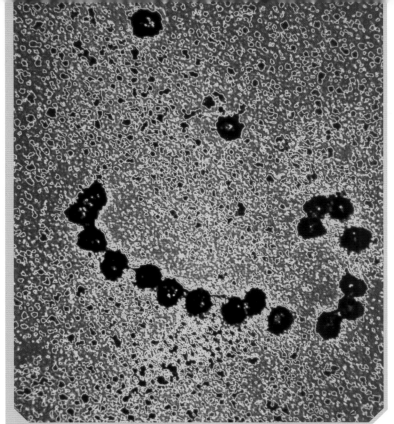

As the ribosome travels along the messenger RNA, a transfer RNA molecule brings the amino acid for a particular codon on the messenger RNA. As each codon is translated, another amino acid is added to the end of the growing polypeptide chain. More than one ribosome can be moving along a messenger RNA molecule at any one time. In this way, there can be polypeptides at different stages of assembly along the messenger RNA strand, just like a factory assembly line.

A photo taken through an electron microscope showing a number of ribosomes (round, colored black) on a single strand of messenger RNA.

At the end of the messenger RNA strand is a special codon called a stop codon. This means "instructions end—stop assembly." The polypeptide chain is complete and is released from the ribosome. It will then fold up, and possibly link with other polypeptides, to form a protein that can go on to fulfill its task in the cell.

Engineering goals

Genetic engineers often try to transfer **genes** from one **organism** to another, or to alter genes within an organism. The point of doing so is to introduce new proteins into the organism, because doing this changes what happens in the cell. Changing the genes is more effective than simply injecting an organism with new proteins. Proteins don't last long, they are broken down and recycled, but once a gene has been written into the **DNA**, its instructions can be read again and again to make new proteins. Since DNA is copied from one generation to the next, from parents to offspring, changes in DNA can be carried over from one generation to the next.

The fact that all organisms use the same genetic code means that we can transfer genes from one species to another, and the new species will be able to read the gene. The universal nature of the genetic code means that any gene can be decoded by any organism and give the same protein product (although there are some problems for bacteria reading **eukaryote** cell genes, as we will see later). Genetic engineers can put human genes in pigs and jellyfish genes in mice.

Gene Control

An **organism's** cells, as we have seen, only use some of their **genes**. Different cell types, with their different tasks to perform, require the services of different **proteins**, which have to be constructed according to the instructions on different segments of the cell **DNA**. Some estimates suggest that the cells of a multi-cellular organism use only 5 to 10 percent of their genes at any given time. This means that there has to be a control system in place that prevents genes from being expressed here, there, and everywhere indiscriminately. A gene that is not expressed has no effect whatsoever on the cell.

Some genes are being expressed all the time because the proteins concerned are involved in vital activities. For instance, the **enzymes** involved in **respiration**, the process by which living things get energy from food, are always needed. Other genes may never be expressed at all in a cell, or may be expressed just once in a while according to need. One reason why bacteria are such phenomenally successful organisms is that they can rapidly increase or decrease the production of enzymes, depending on the nutrients that become available to them.

The genes that code for production of blossoms in these cherry trees are not expressed until environmental factors, such as day length, act as a trigger. This means that all the cherry trees in an area blossom at the same time, making it much easier for trees to pollinate each other.

Regulatory proteins

The control of **gene expression** is very complex. Genes can be turned on or off by special proteins called **regulatory proteins**. Often, several different regulatory proteins can act on one gene. They may act on the gene site itself to allow **transcription**, or they may block it. They may act at a later stage in the process, controlling production of a **polypeptide** by the **ribosomes**. Finally, they may affect the actual polypeptides produced, either activating or deactivating them in some way.

One very simple example of gene regulation was discovered in bacteria more than 30 years ago. A series of genes in the bacteria (lac genes) produce enzymes that can break down the sugar **lactose** (this provides the bacterium with energy). When there is no lactose available, a regulatory protein called a repressor binds to the bacterial DNA and keeps the genes from being transcribed. However, the repressor protein is made inactive by lactose, which keeps the repressor from binding to the bacterial DNA. Therefore, if there is lactose in the bacterial cell, transcription of the lac genes can take place. The lac genes then produce enzymes that the bacterium can use to get energy from the lactose.

A computer graphic showing the (pink) lac repressor protein attached to the DNA. The sites at which it attaches keeps the enzyme RNA polymerase, a promoter, from attaching to the DNA. Magnification approx. x 40,000.

Promoters

Like other reactions in the cell, the production of **messenger RNA** (see illustration on page 7) from a particular stretch of DNA is controlled by an **enzyme**. Before this enzyme can go to work, it must attach to the DNA at a point just before the gene. This site is called a **promoter**. When the enzyme is bound to the promoter site, the gene can be transcribed to produce messenger RNA. Without the enzyme, transcription is not possible.

Unlike the **genetic code** itself, promoters are not universal. Some promoters work in more than one species, but in some cases the enzyme of one species does not recognize and bind to the promoter in another. If this happens, there will be no transcription and no **protein** building: the gene will not be expressed.

If a genetic engineer wants to transfer a gene from one organism to another, the section of DNA they transfer must include the promoter as well as the gene itself. Furthermore, the promoter must be recognized by the binding enzymes in the host organism's cells. If these conditions are not met, nothing will happen.

Some bacteria used in genetic research have enzymes that will readily bind to promoters from a range of other organisms. Other bacteria are very particular about the promoters they will respond to.

3 | Bacterial Benefits

The first successes in genetic engineering involved inserting foreign **genes** into bacteria. This might not seem very useful—bacteria are extremely small, very simple **organisms**. However, genetically engineered bacteria have been useful in several different ways.

These *Bacillus subtilis* bacteria have been genetically modified to produce a vaccine. The red and purple colored areas in the bacteria indicate the presence of the vaccine. Magnification approx. x 50,000.

Humans have a long history of using bacteria for a variety of tasks. Bacteria are involved in the production of yogurt and cheese, for example. We also get **antibiotics**, the drugs we use to fight off infections, from bacteria. Bacteria have been engaged in chemical warfare with one another for many millions of years. Antibiotics are part of this battle. An antibiotic is a substance that kills or prevents the growth of bacteria. Soil bacteria in particular produce antibiotics as part of their natural defenses to kill off other bacterial colonies growing in the same area.

Hundreds of different antibiotics obtained from a variety of **micro-organisms** are in use today. The search for new ones continues as medical science tries to keep pace with the ability of bacteria to evolve rapidly and gain resistance to everything we can throw at them.

Building better bugs

One goal of the genetic engineer is to make bacteria that can do the things we want to do even better. A method used in the past was the hit-and-miss approach of artificially causing **mutations** in a colony of bacteria and hoping that some desirable mutation would occur. A more effective way is to isolate genes that produce **proteins** we are interested in and insert them directly into the bacteria we want to alter. Populations of bacteria grow rapidly, which makes them extremely good chemical factories for the production of useful proteins.

Drugs from bugs

One protein made in genetically engineered bacteria is used to treat **diabetes**. Diabetes is a potentially serious illness caused by an inability to produce a hormone called insulin. Insulin is a protein that is involved in controlling the amount of sugar in the blood. Without it, levels of sugar in the blood can vary wildly, causing many types of problems. In the days before genetic engineering, diabetics were treated with insulin obtained from pigs and cattle. This was not an ideal treatment because insulin from these animals is slightly different from human insulin. Today, stainless steel containers hold large populations of Escherichia coli bacteria (E. coli for short) that have been genetically altered to contain the genes for human insulin. These bacteria were the first large-scale use of genetically engineered organisms. Today, other medically important proteins are also manufactured by bacteria, including blood-clotting agents, growth hormones, and interferon (a protein that is effective against infections caused by **viruses**).

Scientists have still not been able to genetically engineer bacteria to produce antibiotics. Antibiotics are not proteins, so it is not possible to simply insert an antibiotic gene into a bacterium. Instead, genetic engineers would have to insert most or all of the genes that code for the **enzymes** involved in making the antibiotic.

Clean-up squad

Genetically altered bacteria could also be used to deal with pollution. Many bacteria naturally play a role as decomposers, breaking down dead organisms and recycling organic wastes. Naturally occurring bacteria are already being used to help clean up oil spills, and tests are being carried out with others that could be used to deal with toxic chemical leaks. Research is under way to genetically engineer bacteria to increase their ability to deal with these pollutants. Before these bacteria could be used there would have to be absolute certainty that it was safe to do so.

These fermentation containers are used to grow large numbers of micro-organisms that have been genetically altered to produce substances such as insulin.

4 | Inserting New Genes

We have learned about some of the useful jobs that genetically engineered bacteria perform for us. But how exactly are these bacteria made? How do genetic engineers put new **genes** into bacteria?

Introducing *E. coli*

E. coli is a common bacterium that lives in the intestines of mammals, including humans. It is mostly harmless and is very easy to store in the laboratory. In ideal conditions it can divide in two every 40 minutes or so. For many years *E. coli* has been studied by scientists, and the many genetic engineering techniques were developed using this **organism**.

Eukaryote and prokaryote chromosomes

Like all other bacteria, *E. coli* is a **prokaryote**. This means that it has no **nucleus**. The cells of most other living things are **eukaryotes**.

The genetic material in prokaryotes is in some ways different from that in eukaryotes. In eukaryote cells, **DNA** is attached to **proteins** called **histones**. A single molecule of DNA is wound around a number of histones in a complex way, making it compact and able to fit inside the nucleus. The DNA is at its most compact during cell division, when the DNA and histone structure becomes visible under the microscope as a **chromosome**.

In a prokaryote cell, the DNA is naked—it is not enclosed within a nucleus or associated with proteins to form a chromosome. The prokaryote chromosome is simply a DNA molecule folded up inside the cell. The ends of prokaryote DNA molecules are connected to form a closed loop of DNA. Eukaryote chromosomes do not form loops like this.

There are roughly 4 million **base** pairs in the DNA molecule of *E. coli*. This is tiny compared to the 100 million base pairs in a single human chromosome (humans have 23 pairs of chromosomes in each cell). When *E. coli* reproduces, its single chromosome loop is replicated and each new bacterium gets a copy.

A magnified photo of the rod-shaped *E. coli* bacteria. Magnification approx. x 5,000.

Plasmids

In addition to its single DNA molecule, *E. coli* may also have a few smaller loops of DNA called **plasmids**, which can also be passed on at cell division. Plasmids have only a few thousand base pairs. There are various types of plasmid, but generally a bacterium will have only one type at any one time. However, it can have many copies of the same plasmid. It is not unusual for a bacterium to have hundreds of identical plasmids. Sometimes a bacterium can have no plasmids at all, which suggests that plasmids are not essential for the bacterium's survival.

The genes on plasmids are often ones that give the bacterium resistance to **antibiotics**, which bacteria use to wage war on other bacterial strains. A bacterium that has plasmids will be resistant to attack by antibiotic-producing bacteria.

Plasmids are important in genetic engineering because they can be extracted from bacterial cells. They can then be readily introduced into bacterial cells that have no plasmids of their own. Plasmid genes can therefore be introduced into bacteria that previously did not have any.

The discovery of the techniques for transferring plasmids from cell to cell was an important step in the development of genetic engineering, but it was only the beginning. A major factor in the advance of genetic engineering came with the discovery of another weapon that bacteria use to defend themselves against attack. This weapon is a special class of **enzymes** that the bacteria use to chop up the DNA of an attacking **virus**. They are called **restriction enzymes**.

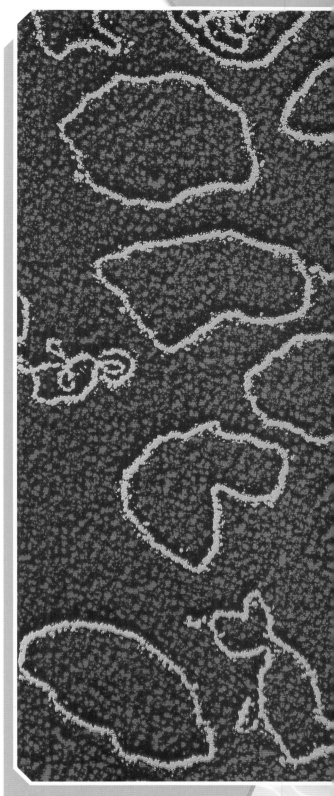

The loops in this photo are plasmids inside an *E. coli* bacterium. Magnification approx. x 80,000.

Chopping up DNA

Multi-cellular animals are vulnerable to attack by **micro-organisms**. This means that they have had to evolve some form of defense against infection. The human **immune system** includes millions of white blood cells, which can identify foreign invaders and then use various methods to deal with them.

A scanning electron micrograph of T4 bacteriophages on an *E. coli* bacterium. The restriction enzymes that bacteria use to cut open viral DNA are used by genetic engineers to cut DNA into fragments. Magnification approx. x 31,000.

Bacteria, though microscopically small, are themselves liable to infection by even smaller disease-causing agents—**viruses**. Viruses that infect bacteria are called **bacteriophages**, often shortened to simply phages. The phages inject their **DNA** into bacterial cells.

Bacteria have a type of defense system to help fight against viral attack, but the bacterial defense system is nothing like our complex immune system. After all, a tiny single-celled **organism** cannot call on millions of white blood cells to attack an invader. Instead, **enzymes** in the bacterium recognize the presence of foreign viral DNA, and other enzymes go to work to chop it into pieces.

The enzymes responsible for chopping up the viral DNA are called **restriction enzymes**. Each type of restriction enzyme recognizes a short sequence of DNA **bases**, called its target sequence. If a foreign DNA molecule has these target sequences, the restriction enzyme will cut through the DNA molecule and split it into fragments. Each fragment is, roughly speaking, a **gene**-sized piece of DNA about 1,000 to 5,000 base pairs in length, just large enough for one or a few genes.

Restriction enzymes and genetic engineering

It is possible to remove restriction enzymes from bacteria and purify them in the laboratory. Many hundreds of enzymes from many strains of bacteria have been isolated, and these make up the genetic engineers' tool kit. They can be used for cutting up DNA, and therefore for cutting out genes. Restriction enzymes make a genetic engineering technique called **recombinant DNA** technology possible. The genetic engineer can use this technique to combine DNA from different species.

Recombinant DNA technology is the basis of genetic engineering. Restriction enzymes are used to cut up the DNA from one organism, and genes of interest are isolated from the fragments. Restriction enzymes are then used to open **plasmids**, and the genes isolated from the first organism are inserted into the opened plasmid. The plasmid is then closed up to produce a plasmid with a foreign gene inserted into it. This technique is called **gene splicing**. Plasmids containing foreign DNA are called recombinant plasmids.

A suspension of bacteria is then treated with the recombinant plasmids.

E. coli containing plasmids

cells of organism containing genes of interest

molecules of DNA

plasmids

open plasmids

pieces of DNA containing genes of interest

insert and splice in pieces of foreign DNA

recombinant plasmids

treatment with chemicals

plasmid-free E. coli

Using restriction enzymes, DNA can be cut into gene-sized fragments. Other enzymes are used to insert the DNA fragments into bacterial plasmids. Bacterial cells are then treated with chemicals to help them absorb the engineered plasmids.

Some of the bacteria absorb the plasmids. The suspension is spread on the surface of a growth medium (a jellylike substance, called **agar gel**, that contains nutrients that the bacteria can use as food), and the bacteria begin to divide. Because the bacteria continue to divide, there will soon be a population of genetically identical individuals, **clones** in other words, all containing a copy of the recombinant plasmid.

The plasmids act as carriers for transferring genes into bacteria. These genes can come from any source. They might come from another bacterium, either of the same or another species, or they might come from an entirely different organism such as a plant or an animal.

Split Genes

When **DNA** and **genes** were first being investigated, it was assumed that each gene was a continuous section of DNA that could be read and transcribed to give a continuous corresponding length of **messenger RNA**. This would then be translated to give the appropriate series of **amino acids** to be linked together in a **polypeptide** chain. However, scientists were surprised to find that the truth was a little more complicated.

There is a major difference between the structure of **eukaryote** genes and **prokaryote** genes. Many genes in eukaryote cells are not a continuous sequence of DNA, but are split over several segments. The DNA is not physically split: the long chain of the molecule remains intact. However, the **protein**-making code that makes up the gene is interrupted by sequences of **bases** that do not code for proteins. These non-coding regions within the gene are called **introns**, because they interrupt the code. The coding regions of the DNA are called **exons**. Not all eukaryote genes are split, but some are split regularly. The gene for collagen, a protein found in animal tissues such as tendons, is interrupted by nearly 40 introns.

Cross-section of an animal cell that has been cultured (grown) in the laboratory. Cells like this are used to produce messenger RNA, from which complementary DNA (cDNA) can be made.

The intron sections of the gene obviously have to be removed before the messenger RNA can be used to manufacture a protein chain. This happens after the messenger RNA has been made from the DNA, but before it leaves the **nucleus**. **Enzymes** cut out the RNA sequences that correspond to the introns and connect the exon sections together again. Once the messenger RNA has been modified, it passes out of the nucleus for translation into a polypeptide.

Bacterial genes have no introns. Each gene is a continuous stretch of DNA code, with no interruptions. This raises a problem for the genetic engineer. If a eukaryote gene is transferred to a bacterium and if that gene happens to be a split gene, there is no way in which the bacterium can produce a protein from that gene. The bacterium has no machinery for modifying RNA and removing introns from it. If genetic engineers want to introduce a eukaryote gene into a bacterium, they first have to find a way of making the split gene usable.

Intron bypass operation

The solution to the problem is to transfer genes that have already had their introns removed. Simply, the eukaryote cells from which the genes are being removed must do most of the work. Rather than cutting up a cell's DNA to get the target gene, the genetic engineer looks for the messenger RNA strand corresponding to the gene in the **cytoplasm** of the cell. Such an RNA strand will already have had the introns removed before leaving the nucleus. Once the messenger RNA has been isolated, it is used as a template to produce a complementary strand of DNA (cDNA). This cDNA strand is equivalent to the gene without its introns.

Copying the RNA to give cDNA is the reverse of what happens during **transcription**: instead of DNA being used to make messenger RNA, messenger RNA is used to make DNA. Scientists can get this reverse transcription to take place in the laboratory thanks to the discovery of an enzyme found in some **viruses**. This enzyme is called, appropriately enough, **reverse transcriptase**.

Reverse transcriptase has a very useful property—when it is brought into contact with a messenger RNA strand and a source of **nucleotides** (the building blocks of DNA), it will assemble a DNA strand that complements the sequence of bases on the RNA. This single DNA strand can then be used as a template to make a second DNA strand, by using the services of another enzyme called **DNA polymerase**. The end result is an artificial gene that contains a continuous sequence of coding bases, without the introns.

The artificial gene can be spliced into a **plasmid**, which can be inserted into a bacterium. Once there, it can start to produce proteins.

How complementary DNA (cDNA) is made, containing only the exons of a eukaryote gene.

Hitting the Target

We have seen how it is possible to move **DNA** from one **organism** to another, but how does the genetic engineer ensure that the correct DNA segment is being introduced? How can specific genes be isolated and transferred?

Dishes of agar gel containing colonies of bacteria that include recombinant genes.

Gene libraries

The complete set of **genes** in an organism is called its **genome**. There are roughly 3,200 genes in the *E. coli* genome, and 20,000 to 25,000 genes in the human genome. When genetic engineers want to isolate a gene, they split up the entire genome of a cell containing that gene, and incorporate the gene fragments into bacteria through **plasmids**. Each of the individual genes from the cell will end up in a separate bacterium. This mixed collection of genetically altered bacteria makes up a gene library of the original organism.

So, we know that the gene we are interested in is somewhere among thousands of genetically modified bacteria, but how do we find it?

Gene screening

The first step in finding the gene we want is to spread the bacteria on a suitable growing medium, such as an **agar gel** containing nutrients. The individual bacteria will then divide, and each one will form a colony containing millions of bacteria. The individuals in each colony will be **clones** of the original bacterium. It is easier to test a colony of clones for a particular gene than it is to attempt to test a single, tiny bacterium.

It is tricky to look for the gene we want to find directly, but it is often possible to look for the **protein** it produces. If the bacteria in a colony are producing a protein, they must have the gene or genes that code for that protein.

If the protein concerned is an **enzyme**, it is reasonably easy to find it. Every enzyme controls a particular chemical reaction in the cell. If we provide each bacterial colony with a sample of the enzyme's **substrate** (the chemical that the enzyme interacts with), we can then test each colony for the products of the reaction.

If the protein product is not an enzyme, there are still ways in which it can be detected. Antibodies are proteins that are produced by the **immune systems** of vertebrates. They are designed to detect foreign proteins and attach to them in order to help neutralize them. Each antibody is specific to a particular intruder, so it is possible to produce antibodies that are specific to a particular protein. The antibody becomes our protein detector. We can use the antibody to screen the bacterial colonies for the protein we want to find.

Gene probes

Another method of finding genes involves the use of **gene probes**. Every type of gene is unique. Each gene has a sequence of **base** pairs found in no other gene, and it is this feature that the genetic engineer uses to identify it. A short stretch of DNA is made that matches a unique part of the gene we are trying to find. This is the gene probe. The probe is labeled using a **radioactive** material. The DNA in the probe will only attach to the gene we are hunting for.

An X-ray plate used in gene probe detection. The dark spots on the plate are fragments of human chromosome 17. A defective version of this gene found on this **chromosome** is associated with breast cancer.

First, a small sample of each colony is transferred to a nylon filter. These sample colonies are then treated with a strong chemical that disrupts the bacterial cells, causing them to release their DNA. The chemical also causes the two strands of each DNA molecule to separate from one another. The filter is treated to remove any traces of protein, and the single-stranded DNA is baked in place. The filter now has DNA prints (sometimes called DNA ghosts) of all the colonies being tested.

To find out which DNA print the probe has bound to, the filter is brought into contact with a sheet of X-ray film. The radioactivity from the label on the probe will cause a dark spot to appear on the film, indicating where the colony we are interested in is located.

Turning to Phages Again

We first met **bacteriophages**, the **viruses** that attack bacteria, when we looked at **restriction enzymes**—the bacterium's defense against virus attack. Restriction enzymes have proven to be a powerful tool for the genetic engineer, but so are the phages themselves, as well as other types of viruses.

Phage delivery systems

Bacteriophages and other types of viruses work by inserting their **DNA** into a host cell, and hijacking the cell machinery to make copies of the virus. The host cell makes copies of the viral DNA, and transcribes the viral genes to make the **proteins** that form the virus's outer coat. The viral proteins and DNA are assembled into new viruses. This is the only way a virus can reproduce—when it is outside a host cell it is basically lifeless.

Genetic engineers can use **phages** as carriers, instead of **plasmids**, to insert foreign DNA into bacterial cells. As with plasmids, restriction enzymes can be used to cut open the DNA and splice in new **genes**. The **recombinant viruses** formed are then used to infect a colony of bacteria. Each phage infects a bacterium and reproduces inside it. The new phages contain copies of the inserted gene. Eventually, the bacterial cell is so full of viral copies that it splits open. The released phages then infect other bacteria in the colony, until there are billions of copies of the recombinant viruses. The viruses containing the genes we are interested in can then be isolated.

One advantage of inserting genes using phages rather than plasmids is that phages can carry longer lengths of foreign DNA than plasmids can. Phages are often used to construct gene libraries because the DNA needs to be split into fewer fragments, meaning that fewer colonies of **clones** need to be made. This makes it easier to find the bacterial colony containing the protein we are looking for.

The DNA of a bacteriophage. Magnification approx. x 50,000.

Other hosts

Although *E. coli* was the first host cell used by genetic researchers, it is certainly not the only one. No cell is immune from virus attack, and viruses can be used to carry foreign DNA into any type of cell, **prokaryote** or **eukaryote**.

It is possible to modify viruses to transfer genes into the host cell's own DNA, instead of making new viruses. When the host cell divides, it not only replicates its own DNA, but also the recombinant viral DNA that has been added to it.

Sometimes a virus can take on a plasmid-like existence inside the host cell, replicating its DNA plus the spliced-in foreign genes independently of the host cell's **chromosomes**. These plasmids are then passed on to the next generation when the host cell divides. No virus particles are produced and the host cell is unharmed.

Stepping up

So far, we have only discussed genetically altering single cells. This is usually done to build microbe factories that will produce a protein that we want to have in large quantities, such as insulin. It might also be done to improve a cell—it might make a bacterium a more efficient consumer of petrochemical wastes, for instance, or alter yeast cells to make them more efficient producers of beer.

This tissue culture of skin provides a way of testing new drugs without using living organisms.

Animal and plant cells can be grown in tissue cultures by taking cells from plant and animal tissues and growing them in the laboratory. These tissue cultures can also be genetically engineered. Animal tissue cultures, for example, are used in the production of **vaccines** for some viruses. However, this is quite different from producing genetically engineered multi-cellular **organisms**. Next, we will look at the techniques involved in producing genetically modified plants and animals.

Going Multi-Cellular

In some ways, the methods used to genetically engineer multi-cellular plants and animals are similar to those used for single-celled **organisms**. Of course, there are differences between the two. A multi-cellular organism is made up of many millions of cells. To change the **genome** of a multi-cellular organism we need to have a way of introducing the new **genes** into every one of its cells in such a way that the new genes are passed on when cell division takes place.

These plantlets of the tobacco plant (*Nicotinia tabacum*) were grown from callus cells. Each callus cell has the potential to form a complete new plant.

We also want the change to be passed on from generation to generation when the organism reproduces. Most living things reproduce sexually, not by simply dividing like a bacterium. This means that offspring inherit their genes from two parents. Each parent forms special sex cells, called **gametes**, with half the number of genes, which combine to form a new organism. Any altered **DNA** needs to be present in these gametes if it is to be passed on to the offspring.

Although each cell in a multi-cellular organism carries the same genes, not all genes are expressed (active) at all times or in all cells. It is therefore important that any introduced genes are in the right place. We would not want the foreign gene to be active unnecessarily, or perhaps not active at all. For example, if we introduced a gene into a plant that improved water uptake by the roots, we would want to avoid having the plant wasting the energy by having its leaves pointlessly producing the protein as well.

Plant regeneration

Plants have a remarkable ability to regenerate themselves. A single cell or small pieces of plant tissue can be persuaded to grow into a whole plant. One way of doing this is from a clump of cells called a **callus**. A callus is a group of **undifferentiated** plant cells—cells that are all the same and have no specialized functions. The cells in a callus are attached to each other;

they are not a colony of single cells, but they can be separated from each other. Given the right conditions, each cell will form a new callus. Each new callus can then be treated with plant hormones and encouraged to grow into a new plantlet. When these plantlets are planted and allowed to grow, they develop into mature plants. Many **clones** of a single plant can be produced in this way.

Producing plant clones in this way has many advantages over growing plants from seeds. Plants with superior characteristics, such as larger fruits, can be cloned in this way. All the clones will share the original plant's characteristics. Although this is one way of taking control of the reproduction of the plant in order to gain a specific result, it is highly selective breeding rather than real genetic engineering.

The advantage of generating plant clones from the genetic engineer's point of view is simple. If we can insert foreign genes into a group of callus cells, then it is reasonably easy to produce genetically altered mature plants from these cells. But there is still the problem of getting the foreign genes into the callus cells. In fact, nature has gotten there ahead of us, and genetic engineers have been able to take advantage of an existing mechanism for getting genes into callus cells.

These round-leaved sundews (*Drosera rotundifolia*) are being grown from tissue cultures in a petri dish. These plants are clones, grown from tiny fragments or single cells of a parent plant in a process called micropropagation. The technique allows quick and easy production of genetically identical plants for agricultural research.

Nature's Genetic Engineer

Many plants, such as potatoes, beans, and most trees can be affected by a condition called crown gall disease. This causes a lump, or **gall**, to appear at the site of a wound. The cause of the disease is a soil bacterium called *Agrobacterium tumefaciens*.

Crown galls on the underside of damaged leaves of a rainforest tree.

A gall is a mass of **undifferentiated** plant cells, like a **callus**. It is like a cancer tumor in a person: a mass of cells growing out of control. Even when the callus is removed from the plant and cultivated in the laboratory away from the bacterium, it remains tumorous. The tumor cells make substances called **opines** that are not found in normal plant cells.

Agrobacterium tumefaciens uses opines as its main nutrient and source of energy. Only this bacterium can make use of opines this way; other soil microbes lack the **enzymes** needed to break down opines. So, only this specific species of bacterium gains an advantage from the plant tumor. When the bacterium infects a plant it genetically engineers the plant cells to produce tumorous cells, which provide it with a source of food.

The return of the plasmids

Agrobacterium tumefaciens uses **plasmids** to cause, or induce, tumors in the plant. These are called **Ti** (tumor-inducing) **plasmids**. The bacterium causes healthy plant cells to change into opine-producing tumor cells by transferring Ti plasmids into them. Once the Ti plasmid has been introduced into the plant cell, part of it becomes integrated into the plant cell's **DNA**. The plasmid DNA transferred to the plant contains **genes** that code for **proteins** involved in gall formation. It also contains another gene that is needed to produce opines. The bacterium has effectively achieved with the plant cells what genetic engineers have been doing with bacteria. It has converted them into factories to produce a product it can use.

It is not too much of a problem for the genetic engineer to copy the success of the *Agrobacterium* in transferring DNA from one species to another. It is a fairly easy procedure to cut out the genes in the plasmid that cause tumor formation and replace them with genes that do things that we want. The genetically altered bacterium is then used to infect plant tissue, and the foreign genes are taken into the plant's DNA as before. It is not necessary to infect every cell in a plant, because entire plants can be regenerated from infected cells in the same way that they are grown from callus cells.

In nature, *Agrobacterium tumefaciens* only infects those plants that belong to the group called dicotyledons, or **dicots**. These are plants that have two leaves, called **cotyledons**, in the seed. They include beans, peas, and potatoes. Many vital food crops, such as rice and wheat, are **monocots** (they have a single seed leaf). Genetic engineers have also succeeded in getting *Agrobacterium* to alter monocots, first with rice and corn, and later with other plants, including wheat, barley, bananas, and pineapples.

Agrobacterium tumefaciens bacteria growing on the surface of tobacco plant cells. These bacteria inject cancer-causing genes into a plant cell. The resulting tumor is destructive to the plant, but is food for the bacteria. Magnification approx. x 26,000.

Activating the new genes

It is not enough just to transfer the genes producing the desired protein into the plant. Plant genes are often controlled by sequences of DNA next to the gene. These sequences need to be included with the gene if it is to be activated in the plant cell. It is possible, by attaching the right control sequences, to have any gene activated in any plant tissue.

Designer Plants

Using *Agrobacterium tumefaciens* is not the only way to get new **genes** into plants. Other means include getting the plant cells to absorb the foreign **DNA** directly, in the same way that bacterial cells can be made to absorb **plasmids**. The difficulty in doing this with a plant cell is that the cell's tough outer wall has to be removed first. This can be done using **enzymes** that break down the cellulose and other materials in the cell wall.

A plant cell with its cell wall removed is called a **protoplast**. Foreign DNA can be introduced into a protoplast using a variety of techniques, such as electric shocks and chemicals. After the new genes have been introduced, the protoplasts will regrow their cell walls (this takes about a week). The plant cells can then be regenerated to create genetically engineered plants.

Better plants

Regeneration has not proven to be as successful with **monocot** cereal plants, such as wheat and corn, as it is with **dicots** such as carrots and potatoes. However, it can be done, and genetically engineered rice, corn, and other crops are now a reality. Improved varieties that give greater yields have been produced.

A grove of golden aspen trees. Aspens are one of the tree species that have been genetically engineered to produce less lignin.

Other plants have been genetically engineered to produce less lignin. Lignin is a tough chemical that strengthens plant cell walls in woody tissues. It must be chemically removed from wood that is used to make paper, so trees engineered to contain less lignin would be very useful to the paper industry.

Plants genetically engineered to be resistant to powerful herbicides (weed killers) are perhaps the most common type of GM (genetically modified) crop. Growing such crops means that farmers can use high levels of herbicides to kill weeds around the crops without harming the crops themselves.

Some people have doubts about the use of genetically modified plants in food. In many countries, research to ensure that such crops are safe is under way.

The tomatoes in the top photo are normal, and have started to get moldy. The tomatoes below them are the same age, but have been genetically modified to be mold-resistant.

Vitamins and vaccines

Genetic engineers are working on the development of plants that can be used to produce medically useful substances such as vitamins, **vaccines**, and human **proteins** such as hemoglobin.

One possibility being explored is to grow plants that have been genetically altered to provide essential vitamins for people in developing countries. Roughly 400 million people worldwide suffer from vitamin A deficiency, which can lead to infections and blindness. Genetic engineers have succeeded in modifying a total of seven genes from plants, bacteria, and fungi and introducing all of them into rice. The result has been to create strains of rice that not only produce the chemical involved in making vitamin A, but also contain large amounts of iron. As little as 300 grams of the cooked, improved rice should provide almost all the vitamin A that a person needs each day.

Another area of research is the development of edible plant vaccines. This could become a simple, cost-effective way to fight disease worldwide. If people could simply eat foods that are part of their normal diet, but are genetically enhanced to carry vaccines, this would avoid the problems and the expense of providing equipment for making, storing, and delivering vaccines in poorer countries where they are most needed. Bananas are one possible carrier for these vaccines. Genetically engineered potato plants that **immunize** a person against bacteria that cause diarrhea have already been successfully grown and tested.

Transgenic Animals

Plants or animals that have been genetically altered using foreign genes are **transgenic organisms**. We have seen what methods have been developed to create transgenic plants. Animals, however, do not have a plant's ability to regenerate from a single cell. So how can transgenic animals be created?

Going to work on the egg

Although adult animals are made up of millions of different cells, every animal starts life as a single cell—the fertilized egg or zygote. As the animal grows, whether inside an eggshell or inside its mother, this single cell divides again and again. As more and more cells are formed, they diversify to produce the various cells and tissues and organs that make up the mature animal. When genetic engineers place a new **gene** or genes into an animal, they want to be sure that every cell in the animal contains the new piece of **DNA**. The simplest way to do this is to add the new DNA to a fertilized egg before it starts to divide. Getting new genes into a fertilized egg involves altering an animal's **gametes** (egg cells in a female, sperm cells in a male). These are the only animal cells capable of creating new offspring. All other cells in an animal are called **somatic cells**. Somatic cells are not capable of regenerating into new animals.

If the altered DNA is successfully incorporated into a **chromosome** in the **nucleus** of a fertilized egg, it will be copied with the rest of the cell's DNA every time the cell divides. The new DNA will thus be present in every cell of the mature animal. The new DNA may also be present in the mature animal's gametes and will be passed on to its offspring.

The fertilized egg cell of a sea urchin. Any changes made to the DNA of a fertilized egg will be present in every cell of the adult organism. Magnification approx. x 1,400.

Micro-injection of DNA into an egg cell. The thick tube on the left is a tiny suction tube that holds the cell in one place. The very fine needle on the right is used to inject DNA into the cell. Magnification approx. x 1,000.

Micro-injection

One way to produce a transgenic animal is to use a technique called **micro-injection**. Injecting DNA into a fertilized egg is a tricky procedure. Using an ultra-fine needle, the new DNA is injected directly into a fertilized egg cell, the zygote, before it starts dividing.

Micro-injection is far from 100 percent effective. In most cases, the injected DNA will not be incorporated into a chromosome in the zygote, and none of the cells in the resulting organism will have the new DNA. Other problems can arise with micro-injection. Sometimes the new DNA does not get incorporated into a chromosome until after the egg has started to divide. The result is a mosaic animal, which contains the new gene in some of its cells, but not in others. Another possibility is that the foreign DNA can disrupt the functioning of an important gene in the host cell, so that the animal is weakened or dies.

Micro-injection of DNA cannot be carried out within the animal: it has to be done in the laboratory. Once the DNA has been injected, each egg has to be implanted into the **uterus** of another female of the same species, who will act as a **surrogate mother**. Only a small number of the implanted eggs will develop successfully into mature, healthy individuals.

The time and effort involved in creating transgenic animals means that we cannot simply produce thousands of mature animals and then test each one to see if it is carrying the genes we are interested in. Instead, the gene we want has to be **cloned** in advance, using bacteria or cell cultures to find the gene. Once we have a supply of cloned cells containing the gene we want, they can be used as a source of the gene for micro-injection.

Transgenic Applications

Researchers have developed **transgenic** animals with inherited diseases that are similar to some of those that affect humans. These animals are used by researchers to study the progress and symptoms of a disease. They can also be used to test potential new drugs and treatments more safely and inexpensively than can be done with human volunteers. The majority of the transgenic animals developed for this purpose are mice, because they are small and easy to manipulate and maintain. However, other animals such as rats, rabbits, and pigs have also been used for disease studies.

Ethics and OncoMouse

In 1988, the DuPont pharmaceutical company was granted a patent in the United States on a transgenic mouse called OncoMouse. This mouse had been altered by giving it certain faulty **genes**, called oncogenes, that made sure it would develop cancer. OncoMice are now used all over the world to test drugs and therapies against cancer.

Other transgenic animals have since been developed for such diseases as **AIDS**, heart disease, and **diabetes**. While the diseases that have been introduced into the mice closely resemble those that appear in humans, there are differences, and this limits the suitability of the mice for research into human cancers. Because of these differences, scientists need to be careful about drawing conclusions on the treatment of a human disease based on the study of transgenic animals.

Although, of course, the scientists involved would say that their studies were carried out with the best of intentions, in other words to rid humans of a terrible disease. There are others who would say that it is wrong to inflict suffering on animals for the benefit of humans. Genetic engineering also raises ethical questions about broader issues such as whether or not we have any right to interfere with nature by designing new **organisms**. The idea of patenting an animal and claiming rights of ownership over it also upsets many people.

This newborn, genetically modified mouse contains jellyfish genes that manufacture a protein called GFP (green fluorescent protein). The GFP makes the mouse glow green. It is hoped that GFP can be used to mark cancer cells in order to study them.

Research in genetics

Transgenic organisms have been developed to allow scientists to study the structure of genes and how they work. They are used to study gene function by seeing what effects specific genetic changes have on the characteristics of the animal. Transgenic zebra fish are used to study how genes are activated during the development of the **embryo**. Human and fish development actually have many similarities, and understanding the embryonic development of this fish can also help with the understanding of human development. Developmental genes in humans have similar functions to those in the zebra fish.

This transgenic mouse is used to study the disease muscular dystrophy. Researchers hope to find the genetic causes of this muscle-wasting disease and to develop a therapy to prevent it.

Drugs, pigs, and spider goats

The drugs that are used to treat some diseases are simply human **proteins**. It is very expensive to obtain these proteins from other humans, and many of them cannot be produced properly by bacteria. For this reason, transgenic animals, which can produce complex human proteins in their milk at relatively little cost, are starting to be used. Transgenic goats have been developed to produce a protein that prevents blood clotting, for example. Other transgenic goats have been given spider genes and now produce *biofilaments*, materials that are as strong as steel, in their milk.

There are many other examples of transgenic animals that could benefit humans. Transgenic pigs grow faster and apparently produce a higher quality of meat than typical ones. These pigs are also more resistant to disease. Transgenic sheep have been developed that produce better wool. Transgenic goats have been bred that produce an antibacterial **enzyme** in their milk. The enzyme combats disease-causing bacteria in the digestive system. Drinking this milk will hopefully give a boost to the **immune systems** of children, especially in the developing world, where illnesses such as diarrhea kill millions every year. There are concerns with the use of transgenic animals, such as the possible consequences if transgenic salmon, farmed for their increased growth rate, were to escape into the wild and breed with wild salmon.

Gene Therapy

Genetic engineering research has now reached the stage where it is possible to alter a person's **genes**. Defects in single genes cause more than 3,000 human diseases. **Gene therapy** is a way of treating, curing, or preventing diseases that result from faulty genes, either by changing the faulty genes themselves or preventing them from being activated. Gene therapy is still in the experimental stage.

If a gene is faulty, then the **protein** it codes for will either be faulty or will not be produced. One way of dealing with a genetic illness is to provide the patient with a supply of the gene product (the protein) that they are lacking. The protein can be made by bacteria genetically engineered to carry a copy of the properly functioning human gene. Giving protein in this way is called **replacement therapy** and it is already widely used. One example of replacement therapy is in people who are born with a faulty gene for a protein called growth hormone. As its name suggests, growth hormone promotes growth. Children with this faulty gene do not grow properly, and without replacement therapy they would be very short as adults. Replacement therapy works well in this instance, because growth hormone affects many areas of the body. However, the growth hormone has to be given by injection over a long period of time. In other genetic diseases replacement therapy is of limited value, because of the difficulty of targeting the specific cells affected by the illness.

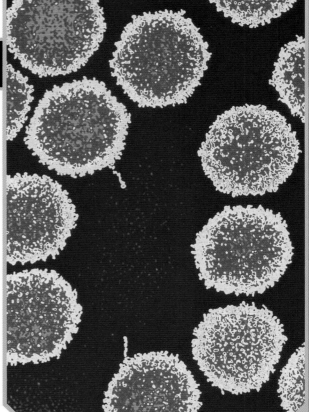

These viruses have been genetically modified to contain the CFTR gene. A faulty CFTR gene is responsible for the disease cystic fibrosis. Researchers try to use the viruses to give cystic fibrosis patients the correct CFTR gene. Magnification approx. x 250,000.

Somatic and germ-line therapies

Gene therapy is a much more direct approach to dealing with genetic illnesses. Rather than replacing the protein product, gene therapy attempts to replace the faulty gene. It can be targeted either on **somatic** (body) **cells**, or on germ cells. In somatic gene therapy, the patient's **DNA** is altered, but not in such a way that the change is passed on to the next generation. In germ-line gene therapy, egg and sperm cells are changed, with the goal of passing on the changes to the offspring. Germ-line gene therapy is controversial because it would mean allowing new genes to enter the human gene pool.

Many problems stand in the way of developing successful gene therapy techniques. One of these is finding a reliable way of getting the replacement gene into the body's cells. Currently, the most common means of doing so is to use **viruses**. Viruses, as we have seen, can be engineered to deliver packages of genes into cells. Viruses are an effective way of adding genes into cells, but there can be problems because the body's **immune system** may still recognize the viruses as invaders. This triggers inflammation and other disease responses.

Researchers are also experimenting with other approaches. One is to introduce an artificial **chromosome** into the body's cells. It would take its place alongside the normal chromosomes and would not interfere with them or cause any **mutations**. It would be capable of carrying substantial amounts of **genetic code**, and would not be attacked by the immune system.

Trials in humans

Another problem is in knowing what specific genes do. There are roughly 25,000 genes in the human **genome** and scientists know the function of only a few. Genes may have more than one function if they work together with other genes, and some genetic illnesses are caused by more than one gene. There is also the difficulty of targeting specific cells. In 2003, French researchers reported the successful treatment of four boys suffering from a deficiency in their immune systems. But within a few months it was discovered that some of the genes had been delivered to the wrong places, and two of the boys had developed leukemia.

In 2006, scientists at the National Institutes of Health in Bethesda, Maryland, successfully treated two patients suffering from a type of cancer by genetically altering the body's killer T cells (part of the immune system) so that they would attack the cancer cells.

The world's first surgical gene therapy procedure for Parkinson's disease was carried out in 2003. A virus was used to alter the genes in a group of cells that were causing the impaired movement associated with Parkinson's.

Stem Cells

Stem cells are **undifferentiated cells** that can divide indefinitely and can give rise to more specialized tissue cells. A fertilized human egg cell is a type of stem cell that is described as being **totipotent**, meaning that its potential is total—it has the potential to form an entire **organism**. In the first hours after fertilization, this cell divides into two identical totipotent cells. About four days after fertilization and after several more cell divisions, these totipotent cells begin to specialize. They form a hollow sphere of cells called a **blastocyst**.

A human embryo at the blastocyst stage, six days after fertilization. Some of the blastocyst cells will form the placenta, others will form the embryo itself. Magnification approx. x 1,500.

The outer layer of the blastocyst forms the **placenta**, which nourishes the **embryo** in the **uterus**. The inner layer of the blastocyst forms the many different tissues of the embryo. Although the cells in the inner layer of the blastocyst can form the embryo, they cannot give rise to the placenta. These cells are now said to be **pluripotent**—they can give rise to many, but not all types of cells.

The pluripotent stem cells become more specialized and give rise to cells that have a specific function. Blood stem cells develop into red blood cells, white blood cells, and platelets (disc-shaped cell fragments that are important for blood clotting), for example. These more specialized stem cells are called **multipotent**.

Multipotent stem cells are found in the body throughout life. Their job is to replace cells lost through natural wear and tear. For example, blood stem cells are found in the bone marrow and in very small numbers in the bloodstream. Their job is to produce new red blood cells, white blood cells, and platelets to replace worn out cells.

Using stem cells

Stem cells could be used in numerous ways. One exciting possibility is that embryonic stem cells could be used as universal human donor cells, able to provide new liver cells, heart cells, or nerve cells to replace tissues that have been lost or damaged. It may also be possible to treat diseases such as **diabetes**, **Parkinson's disease**, and **Alzheimer's disease**.

Embryonic stem cells could also be used to provide a source of normal human cells of virtually any tissue type for use in drug screening. Embryonic stem cells seem to be immortal when grown in the laboratory—they keep dividing again and again, without aging.

These are blood stem cells from human bone marrow. Magnification approx. x 6,800.

Obtaining stem cells

Fertility clinics routinely store frozen embryos in order to help women who have difficulties in having children. These embryos could be used as a source of stem cells, but obtaining cells in this way is highly controversial, because for many people each embryo represents a potential human life.

Toward the end of 2006, scientists began to use cells from embryos that had stopped developing and might be considered dead. Some researchers maintain that too little is known about the way embryos develop to be sure that one really is dead. Another problem is that if there was something wrong with the embryo, something might be wrong with the cells, and that could cause problems with their use.

Another, less controversial, source of stem cells is from the blood in the umbilical cords of newborn infants. In October 2006, scientists at Newcastle University in the United Kingdom, working with colleagues from NASA in Houston, Texas, succeeded for the first time in getting umbilical cord stem cells to grow into liver cells. These cells could be used in the testing of new drugs, which would cut down on animal testing and possibly hazardous tests on human volunteers.

Making Clones

Clones are a group of **organisms** that are genetically identical. Many such organisms in nature result from **asexual reproduction**, in which a new organism develops from only one parent. Strawberries and other plants that grow from runners are genetically identical to the parent plant, for example. Gardeners often use techniques such as cutting and grafting to produce clones of plants. All the offspring of a single parent are clones. Identical twins are also clones: both twins develop from the same fertilized egg.

Identical twins are natural clones. Identical twins are formed if a fertilized egg cell splits in two, and both cells grow and develop separately.

The clone arrangers

In 1997, researchers in Scotland produced the world's first cloned mammal, Dolly the sheep. Dolly was created using a technique called **somatic cell** nuclear transfer. Genetic material is transferred from the **nucleus** of an adult donor cell to an egg from which the nucleus, containing its genetic material, has been removed. The egg containing the donor cell **DNA** is treated with chemicals or electric current to begin cell division. Once the cloned **embryo** has grown to a certain size, it is transferred to the womb of a female sheep where it continues to develop until birth.

Transferring the nucleus works, because somehow the **genes** in the donor cell's nucleus are all activated so the adult cell acts like a **stem cell** instead of, say, an udder cell. Until then, scientists had believed that once a cell became specialized the unnecessary genes in the cell became permanently inactive. Some believe that errors in this process are the cause of the high rates of death and disability seen in animal clones. Dolly died in 2003, suffering from arthritis and lung cancer, but it is uncertain whether or not these conditions resulted from the fact that she was a clone.

Five genetically engineered sheep clones. These clones were not made by micro-injection, like Dolly. Instead, a normally fertilized egg was removed from the sheep after only a few divisions. The cells that had formed from the initial egg cell were then separated and placed in **surrogate mothers**.

Practical cloning

Other uses of cloning that have been suggested include the mass production of animals engineered to carry human genes for the production of **proteins** for use as drugs. The mass production of animals with genetically modified organs to be used as transplant organs for humans is another possibility, as is the mass production of livestock that have been genetically modified to possess desirable characteristics, such as high milk yield in cows. Cloning could perhaps also be used to save endangered species, although the result would be a genetically weak population because there would be very little genetic diversity.

Send in the clones?

The appearance of Dolly raised the possibility of a troubling scenario: that humans might be cloned too. Cloning is an uncertain procedure—Dolly was one success out of more than 270 attempts. While some animals have been cloned successfully, others, including dogs, horses, and monkeys have not. Even when cloning succeeds, it can result in an animal that is more likely to get an infection, has poor health, and dies at an earlier age than normal. Researchers studying cloned mice discovered that many of their genes were not working properly—not because of **mutations**, but because they were not being activated correctly. Cloned animals can simply die for no apparent reason.

Cloning humans may be possible in theory, but as we can see from our experience with animals, there are enormous risks involved. In addition, animal studies can give us no indication of how a cloned human would develop intellectually. For these reasons, most responsible scientists are opposed to human cloning.

A Genetic Map

In 1990, a giant international research program called the Human Genome Project decided to try to identify all of the approximately 25,000 **genes** in human **DNA**—the human **genome**—and to determine the sequence of the 3 billion or so **base** pairs that make up human DNA. Rapid advances in technology sped up the process. By 2000, a working draft covering 90 percent of the genome had been completed, and by 2003 rough drafts of the entire genome had been sequenced, two years ahead of schedule. In May 2006, researchers announced the completion of the DNA sequence for all 24 human **chromosomes**.

As well as mapping human DNA, researchers have also sequenced the genomes of several other **organisms**, including *Escherichia coli*, the fruit fly, and the mouse. Even species as seemingly different from us as yeast and fruit flies share many similar genes. Valuable information about human diseases can be gained by studying the role of a similar gene in the fruit fly. For example, the role of some human genes in cancer is better understood because scientists have studied related genes in flies. In these studies, they found that many of these cancer genes are involved in guiding the development of the **embryo**.

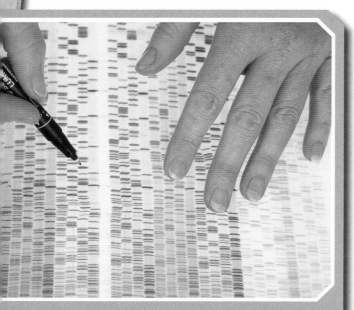

A scientist marking reference points on an X-ray showing DNA sequences. The reference points allow scientists to figure out how different sections of the sequence fit together, like pieces of a puzzle.

The information gained by mapping the genome has been invaluable to geneticists working on genetic illnesses. For example, by 1989 geneticists had tracked down only four genes associated with disease by laboriously sorting through inheritance links between sufferers. The gene for **cystic fibrosis** was found in 1989, after a nine-year search. In 1997, the gene for **Parkinson's disease** was identified in just nine days, and described accurately within nine months. Tests are now available for more than 900 genetic illnesses.

Researchers can electronically scan long stretches of DNA to find genes in the sequence that may be responsible for a particular disease. Those are called **candidate genes**. If a candidate gene actually does play a role in a disease, the sequence of its base pairs should be different in people with the disease. This difference can be minor. Parkinson's disease can result from a change in just a single base pair, which means that just one of the 140 **amino acids** that make up a key **protein** is altered to prevent the protein from doing its job.

Cystic fibrosis

Knowing the DNA sequence of a gene, and therefore the sequence of the amino acids it codes for, sometimes allows researchers to deduce the shape and possibly the function of the protein produced. For instance, when scientists discovered the gene for cystic fibrosis, they recognized it as coding for one of the proteins that are embedded in the membrane of a cell. These proteins act as gateways that allow certain substances to pass in and out of the cell. It also seemed likely that the protein's task was to allow chloride ions to pass out of the membrane. In cystic fibrosis this protein no longer works correctly, which has wide-ranging results. Digestive **enzymes** clog a duct between the pancreas and the small intestine, and food can no longer be digested properly. Thick mucus builds up in the respiratory tract, which can cause repeated lung infections. Cysts (sac-like swellings) form in the pancreas, and it becomes fibrous in appearance (hence the name of the disease). Cystic fibrosis is the most common genetic illness affecting Caucasians (white people), and is always fatal.

Although no cure has been found for cystic fibrosis, scientists are investigating an exciting possibility. Instead of trying to repair the damaged gene, this technique involves using a modified **virus** to repair the **messenger RNA** produced by the gene.

Uncovering the complete sequence of the human genome was a remarkable achievement, but it was only a beginning. Researchers are now trying to understand how each gene functions, and are studying how the proteins they code for work together in each organism.

A laboratory worker loads DNA samples into a machine that automatically processes the samples and determines their DNA sequences. A large amount of computing power is needed to store the thousands of different DNA sequences and to find patterns that ma it possible to fit them together.

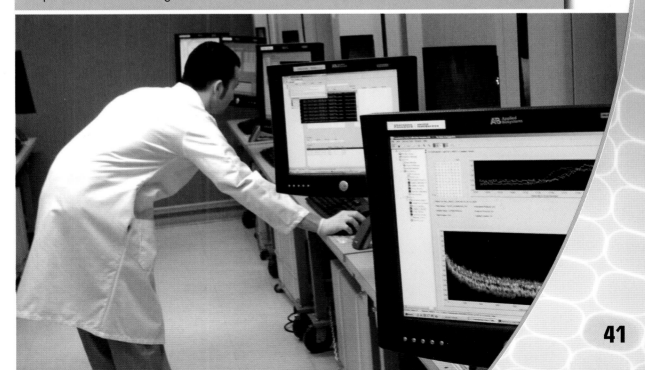

Genome Challenges

The ambitious international Human **Genome** Project has been a resounding success. Many other **organisms** have also had their genomes completely sequenced. How much can we expect our knowledge of the **genes** that make us human to change our lives, if at all? One certain result will be a much greater understanding of biology. Genetic knowledge is already proving useful in developing more effective treatments for many diseases.

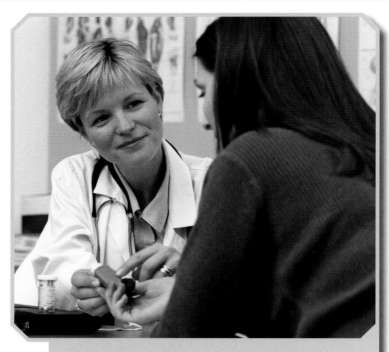

In the future, a doctor or hospital treating a patient will have the enormous advantage of detailed information about the patient's genetic makeup.

Pharmacogenomics

Pharmacogenomics is the science of using genetic information to predict the safety and effectiveness of a drug. In the future, a person's medical records may include the complete **base** sequence of their genome and a catalog of their genes. It will be possible to use this genetic information to predict how that person will respond to certain drugs and to other substances such as pollutants in the environment. This means it will be possible to treat each person as a unique genetic individual. Medical treatments will be more specifically tailored to the individual and will have a greater chance of success. In addition, each person will know their genetic weaknesses. This will give them the chance to change their lifestyle to avoid developing illnesses such heart disease or allergies to certain foods.

Many people die every year from bad reactions to drugs, and millions more suffer uncomfortable side effects. As genes that influence drug response are identified, the number of these bad reactions should be greatly reduced. Drug treatments often fail because the patient lacks the gene that allows the body to use the drug effectively. Knowing in advance whether or not this will happen would give doctors and patients the ability to avoid wasting time and money on ineffective treatments and go right to the drug with the best chance of working.

Life, but not as we know it?

There are also some troubling consequences of knowing more about individual genetic differences. It is not too hard to imagine a society in which the **DNA** of every newborn child is mapped and stored in a giant computer database. It is already possible to use a process called DNA fingerprinting to tell with almost complete certainty whether two samples of DNA are from the same person. Police use this technique to check whether small amounts of DNA (such as from a person's skin) found at a crime scene match the DNA of a suspect. If everyone's DNA sequence was already stored in a computer database, it would be easier to match the DNA from a crime scene to a name on the database. However, many people would feel strongly that holding such information on them would be a restriction to their personal freedom.

This forensic scientist is checking the evidence from a crime scene for DNA. DNA fingerprints can prove conclusively whether or not a particular person committed the crime.

There is also the possibility that people's genetic information would be made available to insurance companies or employers. Insurance companies might charge more to insure people who are more likely to get specific diseases. They could do this even though the person wasn't sick at the time. Employers might even avoid hiring people who could possibly fall seriously ill in the future.

Genetic engineers already have the knowledge to create synthetic genes by splicing together DNA **nucleotides**. As our knowledge of genes and development increases, it may become possible for scientists to create from scratch, in the laboratory, a fully functioning living cell. This might seem like an exciting prospect, but it also raises serious concerns. Do we really know enough about living things and how they work to be sure about creating what would effectively be a new form of life?

Genetic engineering can have immense benefits, but it can also cause serious problems. The more that we understand about the uses and the limitations of genetic engineering, the better we will be at making the difficult decisions about what kinds of genetic engineering we would like to see, and what is not acceptable.

Some Major Events in Genetics

1856	Austrian monk and botanist Gregor Mendel starts his breeding experiments on peas (that will lead him to create the laws of heredity)
1858	English naturalists Charles Darwin and Alfred Russel Wallace announce the theory of Natural Selection: individuals that are better adapted to their environment survive, reproduce, and pass on their characteristics
1859	Darwin publishes *The Origin of Species*
1866	Mendel publishes the results of his investigations on inheritance in pea plants
1871	Nitrogen and phosphorus material discovered in cell nuclei, now known as the genetic material DNA
1873	First accurate description of mitosis
1900	Mendel's principles were independently discovered by several scientists, and verified, marking the beginning of modern genetics
1902	Chromosomes identified as carriers of genes when cell division is shown to be connected with heredity
1920s	Major component of chromosomes is shown to be DNA
1944	Role of DNA in genetic inheritance is first demonstrated by U.S. biologist Oswald Avery
1953	U.S. biologist James Watson and English molecular biologist Francis Crick announce the three-dimensional structure of the DNA molecule as a double helix. They also propose a mechanism for replication of DNA
1954	U.S. cosmologist George Gamow suggests that the genetic code consists of the order of triplets of bases in the DNA molecule
1956	Humans shown to have 23 pairs of chromosomes
1958	U.S. geneticists show that genes act by regulating definite chemical events in the cell
1966	It is shown that DNA has triplet codons that specify each of the 20 amino acids
1969	U.S. geneticists isolate a single gene for the first time
1973	Technique of recombinant DNA developed by U.S. scientists. This marks the beginning of genetic engineering
1981	Insulin made by bacteria is the first genetically engineered product to go on sale
1984	Genetic fingerprinting technique of identifying individuals (the DNA pattern is unique to each person) developed by British geneticist Alec Jeffreys
1988	Human Genome Project begun, with the goal of determining the entire sequence of bases in human DNA
1990	First successful gene therapy carried out in the United States for a girl with SCID—a rare immunodeficiency disease caused by a genetic defect
1993	Flavr Savr tomatoes, the first genetically engineered food (for longer shelf-life), are marketed
1997	Scottish geneticists at the Roslin Institute clone a sheep (named Dolly)
1999	Complete base sequence of human chromosome 22 announced: there are more than 500 genes
2000	The Human Genome Project presents its preliminary map of the 3.1 billion base units that make up human DNA. We may have fewer than 30,000 genes
2003	The Human Genome Project is successfully completed more than two years ahead of schedule

Glossary

agar gel jellylike substance made from seaweed, which is used as a growth medium for bacteria

AIDS (acquired immune deficiency syndrome) viral disease that seriously damages a person's immune system

Alzheimer's disease disease that causes memory loss, poor mental ability, and eventually physical problems

amino acid naturally occurring chemical used by cells to make proteins

antibiotics chemicals that destroy or stop the growth of disease-causing bacteria

asexual reproduction reproduction in which an organism produces genetically identical copies (clones) of itself

bacteriophage (phage) virus that infects bacteria

base type of chemical found in genetic material. There are four different bases in DNA.

blastocyst hollow, fluid-filled ball of cells, an early stage in the growth of a fertilized human egg

callus growth of unspecialized cells that forms in a plant over a wound

candidate gene gene that has been identified as possibly the site of a particular genetic disease

catalyst substance that speeds up a chemical reaction. Enzymes are the catalysts of biological reactions.

chromosome DNA molecule coiled around protein molecules called histones. Chromosomes are present in the nuclei of eukaroyte cells. During nuclear division, they become visible as rodlike structures.

clones organisms that are genetically identical to each other

codon sequence of three bases on RNA molecules that together code for a particular amino acid

cotyledons structures in a plant seed that become the plant's first leaves, or act as a food store

cystic fibrosis disease caused by a faulty gene that involves large amounts of mucus production, especially in the lungs, leading to repeated lung infections

cytoplasm all the contents of a cell outside the nucleus

deoxyribonucleic acid *see* DNA

diabetes disease caused by a lack of the hormone insulin, in which there is no control over the levels of sugar in the blood

dicot (dicotyledon) type of plant that has two cotyledons or seed leaves. Roses, dandelions, and violets are common dicots.

DNA (deoxyribonucleic acid) genetic material of living things. DNA carries instructions for constructing, maintaining, and reproducing living cells.

DNA polymerase enzyme that is involved in replicating one strand of DNA from another

embryo very young organism in the early stages of development, before it emerges from the egg or seed, or is born from its mother's uterus

enzyme type of protein that controls one of the thousands of chemical reactions inside a living cell

eukaryote one of the two basic types of cells. All types of living things, except the archaea and bacteria, are made up of eukaryote cells.

exons stretches of DNA that code for a protein

gall swelling produced on a plant caused by the attack of a parasite. Crown galls are caused by the bacterium *Agrobacterium tumefaciens*.

gametes sex cells in organisms that reproduce sexually. During sexual reproduction a male and a female gamete fuse (join) to form a new organism.

gene stretch of DNA that contains the information to make all or part of a protein

gene expression production of a protein from a gene or genes. When a gene is expressed (activated) it gives rise to characteristics in the organism, such as pink flowers in a pea plant, or curly hair in a child.

gene probe short stretch of DNA whose sequence of bases matches up with a unique part of a particular gene. The probe is tagged with radioactivity, and can be used to find a specific gene.

gene splicing process of cutting open a DNA molecule, inserting a new gene or genes, and then closing it up again

gene therapy treatment for a genetic disease that tries to replace a faulty gene with one that works properly

genetic code way in which the four bases that make up DNA or RNA chains code for the 20 amino acids that make up proteins. Each set of three bases codes for one amino acid or a stop codon.

genome complete set of genetic information of a particular individual

histones proteins in the cell nucleus that are closely associated with DNA

immune system system that protects an organism from infection and disease

immunize to protect a person against a specific illness by stimulating their immune system

introns sections of a gene in a eukaryote cell that do not code for a protein or part of a protein

lactose complex sugar made of galactose and glucose

messenger RNA molecule that carries the genetic code for a protein from the nucleus to the ribosomes, where protein assembly takes place

micro-injection use of an ultra-fine needle to inject DNA into a cell

micro-organisms single-celled organisms that are too small to be seen with the naked eye

Glossary

monocot type of plant that has one cotyledon or seed leaf. Tulips, grasses, and cereals such as wheat are common monocots.

multipotent cell that is capable of giving rise to a number of different cell types

mutation any change in a cell's genes or in a chromosome's structure, or a change in the number of chromosomes in a cell

nucleotides small molecules that join together in chains to form DNA and RNA molecules

nucleus biggest and most obvious structure inside a eukaryote cell. The nucleus is where the cell's genetic material is stored.

opines substances made by tumor cells in plants

organism any type of living thing

Parkinson's disease disease of the nervous system in which the muscles become rigid and the patient cannot move

phage *see* bacteriophage

placenta structure produced by the fertilized egg in mammals, which connects to the uterus and obtains nutrients for the growing baby from the mother's blood

plasmid small, circular piece of DNA found in many bacteria. Plasmids often give bacteria resistance to an antibiotic.

pluripotent cell that is capable of producing all the different cells in a human or mammal, except for the placenta

polypeptide large number of amino acids joined together to form one long molecule. A protein consists of one or more polypeptides.

prokaryote simplest type of living cell. Archaea and bacteria are prokaryotes; all other living things are made up of eukaryote cells.

promoter section of DNA immediately before a gene, where the enzyme responsible for producing messenger RNA for that gene attaches

proteins substances that make up many cell parts and control a cell's reactions. Proteins are large molecules made up of many subunits called amino acids.

protoplast plant cell without its cell wall

radioactive substance whose atoms gradually break down, emitting some kind of radiation (high-energy waves or subatomic particles)

recombinant DNA DNA from one source containing some material from another source, such as viral DNA containing a human gene

recombinant virus virus containing DNA from another source within its own DNA

regulatory proteins proteins that are involved in controlling whether or not a gene is expressed or activated

replacement therapy treatment for a genetic disease in which a protein that is lacking due to a faulty gene is injected into the patient

respiration process by which living things obtain oxygen from the environment to be used in the breakdown and release of energy from their food

restriction enzymes enzymes that cut DNA molecules at specific points, breaking them up into fragments

reverse transcriptase enzyme that makes it possible to make a DNA molecule from an RNA template

ribonucleic acid *see* RNA

ribosomes small structures within cells that are the sites of protein synthesis

RNA (ribonucleic acid) substance related to DNA that plays an important role in protein synthesis

somatic cell any cell in a multicellular organism that is not a reproductive cell (a gamete)

stem cell nonspecialized cell that can divide to form several or many different cell types

substrate substance on which an enzyme acts

surrogate mother female that incubates and gives birth to an embryo that is not her own

Ti plasmid small, circular piece of DNA found in the bacterium *Agrobacterium tumefaciens* that causes a plant to grow a gall

totipotent stem cell that is capable of dividing and growing to produce a complete organism

transcription the production of a single-stranded RNA molecule from a section of DNA

transfer RNA type of RNA that is involved in carrying amino acids to the ribosomes and in attaching them to protein chains

transgenic organism organism containing a gene or genes from another organism

translation process by which information coded on messenger RNA is transformed into a protein

undifferentiated cell that has not become specialized for a specific task

uterus organ in a female mammal where its offspring develop before birth

vaccine substance, often dead or inactivated disease-causing micro-organisms, that stimulates the immune system and gives immunity to a disease

virus small section of DNA or RNA surrounded by a protective protein coat, which can infect a living cell and cause it to produce copies of the virus

Further Reading and Websites

Books

Farndon, John. *From DNA to GM Wheat*. Chicago: Heinemann Library, 2007.

Morgan, Sally. *From Mendel's Peas to Genetic Fingerprinting*. Chicago: Heinemann Library, 2006.

Morgan, Sally. *Genetic Engineering (Moral Dilemmas)*. Mankato, Minn.: Smart Apple Media, 2003.

Parker, Steve. *Genetic Engineering (Face the Facts)*. Chicago: Heinemann Library, 2005.

Rooney, Anne. *Medicine: Stem Cells, Genes, and Superbeams*. Chicago: Heinemann Library, 2006.

Websites

Cells Alive (www.cellsalive.com)
> A good introduction to the cell, with homework help.

Cloning Fact Sheet (www.ornl.gov/sci/techresources/Human_Genome/elsi/cloning.shtml)
> Information on cloning from the Human Genome Project.

DNA from the Beginning (www.dnaftb.org/dnaftb/1/concept)
> Ideas about, DNA, genes, and inheritance.

Eureka Science (www.eurekascience.com/ICanDoThat/index.htm)
> A quirky guide to the way cells and DNA work.

Genetics Home Reference (http://ghr.nlm.nih.gov)
> A guide to genes, genetic conditions, and gene therapies.

How Stuff Works—Cells (www.howstuffworks.com/cell.htm)
> Worth a visit to discover unusual aspects of life at cell level.

The Basics and Beyond (http://learn.genetics.utah.edu/units/basics/index.cfm)
> University of Utah guide to the science of genetics.

The Human Genome Project (www.ornl.gov/sci/techresources/Human_Genome/home.shtml)
> All about the project to map out the human genome.

Index